FRIDAY
and the Year That Followed

FRIDAY
and the Year That Followed

Poems by Juan J. Morales

Winner of the 2005 Rhea & Seymour Gorsline Poetry Competition

FAIRWEATHER BOOKS • BROWNSVILLE, OREGON

First Edition 2 3 4 5 6 7 8 9

Library of Congress Cataloging in Publication Data
Juan J. Morales,
Friday and the Year That Followed
ISBN 13: 978-0-9771973-5-4
ISBN 10: 0-9771973-5-2
Library of Congress Control Number: 2006934949

Fairweather Books is an imprint of
Bedbug Press
P.O. Box 39
Brownsville, OR 97327
www.bedbugpress.com

Cover Art: *Paisaje de Quito* by Oswaldo Guayasamín
    By permission of Fundación Guayasamín, Quito, Ecuador
Author Photo: Lauren Morales
Design: Cheryl McLean

Printed by Thomson-Shore, Inc., Dexter, MI.

This book is printed on acid-free paper.

ACKNOWLEDGMENTS

Some of these poems first appeared or are forthcoming as follows:

Blue Mesa Review: "Chorizo's Father"

Borderlands: The Texas Poetry Review: "Patapalo the Imbecile"

Poet Lore: "In the Earthquake of 1949," "Digging out the Church"

War, Literature, & the Arts: "Siren," "Minesweep on Highway 13 near Lai Key," and "The Cloverleaf"

For Lauren,
my father, and my mother,
who gave me these stories

CONTENTS

I: AMBATO

II: THE GREEN GOLONDRINA

III: WANDERING BETWEEN VILLAGES

Friday, it was Friday
when Jesus died on the cross.
Juan said, I am afraid, Lord.
Then Jesus said,
There is no fear, nor fright
for he who says this prayer
three times when going to bed
and three times upon getting up.
His enemy will never see him,
and he will find
the doors of heaven open.

—The Prayer for Sleep

I: AMBATO

FRIDAY AND THE YEAR THAT FOLLOWED

Ambato, Ecuador, 1949

We never saw him before that Friday.
I was ten when the hollowed man
came to our house. He was tall,

dark-skinned, but not like los indígenas,
who sold crafts on the street,
washed clothes in the withering river.

Mamá eased against the wood door, eager
to make him go. His shadow turned,
looked at me. He stared past her as if he entered.
I felt the man everywhere: he creeped

up the leg of the kitchen table,
stood in corners, and brushed past us
light as breath we blew on hot soup.

My tingling skin, hairs on my neck told me
this year would hold my eyes open. Mamá kissed
my forehead, told me to pray,

For the man with no blood came for you.
Sunrays faded, became slivers.
The mountains and town grew cold as rings
left on the table from the soup.

When everyone went to bed,
all the lights snuffed, creaking floors halted,
and I knew the tall man was there.

He walked through rooms, eating sleep
from my body, and touched our belongings,
like the other ghosts lost in Ambato.

ALL THE JOKES ABOUT GHOSTS

I lay in bed staring at the ceiling
when the bee came to me, wings
drumming against its body.
Two feet long, with no stinger,

the bee flew dizzy circles,
refusing to disappear.
Behind the antennae, mosaic eyes
scared all sleep and dream

out of me. I lay still, unable
to shut my eyes. My sisters slept;
the prayer mother taught us
could not pass my throat.

I knew the bee was a soul in limbo.
When the sun began its rise,
I misplaced it in walls and light.
I kept thinking about how we laughed
at stories of spirits, who, like the bee,
fed on children's sleep.

THE DOGS WHO BREATHED FIRE

1935

The large dogs nobody believes in
are chasing my grandfather.

He runs along the trail into town
between eucalyptus trees.

Looking back, he sees streaks of fur
in darkness. The black dogs sniff air,

growling. Paws strike ground,
and fire comes through their throats.

My grandfather shrieks at the heat
on his heels; the dogs vanish

at the town's edge.
Remnants of smoke drift into the trees.

When he wakes the neighborhood,
the families listen to him

the way they hear whiskey-soaked stories
roll from the mouths of los barachos.

Sweat cools his skin, lungs tremble
like the laughter of neighbors who shrug

and return to their beds, leaving him
to stutter, to pant, to remember charred air

and swallowed fire fading
in the cavernous mouths of the forest.

WHEN MY FATHER HAD LA VIRUELA

1946

We did not see our father
for months. My brothers told me he
had become a monster allergic to light.
Every night, I heard him leave

his walled-up room, where Mamá hid him
from the government quarantined camps
where the infected died. Once, I sneaked

out of bed, watched him at the table
eat cold rice and a chicken slab. It never
left me, the scrape of his fork against
the plate, the long breaths he drew

between bites, the image of our father—
a thing hunched over his meal.
His hands, arms, and face swelled
with tight purple blisters. Before he finished,

I slipped back into bed between my sisters.
Candlelight interrupted darkness
when he stopped in front of our room

and nudged the door open to look at us.
I closed my eyes, held my breath,
and listened to the clap
of his bare feet vanish into the walls.

PROPHETIC

Mamá dreamed of the earthquake
the night before it happened:
she looked into an empty room,
noticed me pressed against the wall
under the left arm of the ceramic Christ.

His head rested downward,
eyes sheltered by shadow.
Light angled through thorns,
shined on the blood and skin.
Mamá's eyes followed me
as I tried to slide my small body

downward, away from the crucifix.
The house shook; cracks snaked
up the walls, dust in the air.
Before Mamá woke up, she whispered
to me, *You are protected.*

EN LA IGLESIA MATRIZ

The twin Buenaño sisters
argued and cursed in La Matriz
just after the first tremors
emptied the church.
The priest and parishioners
in line for confession
heard them both promise
to be happy and wear
a red dress to the other's funeral.

The priest didn't understand
how much these women hated each other,
how their hard eyes could bully him
through tiny squares in the divider
of the confessional. Leaning into the screen,
the priest nodded and listened.
He pushed his glasses
along his nose and forgave.

When the earthquake really started,
the pillars of the church fell:
bricks, statues, stained glass.
Heavy dust covered splintered pews.
The Buenaño sisters and the priest
died with the rest on First Friday.
The remaining wall stood above
them and the still-intact gold altar
with three windows, three armless saints.

IN THE EARTHQUAKE OF 1949

I.

We wait to return to the church
once the earthquake stops.
I'm the last in the group of girls
following the nun back in for catechism.
When my feet touch the steps, I pause.
Flocks of pigeons burst into the sky.
The earth rumbles again, then fractures.

Inside the church, pools of holy water
seep through cracks,
columns snap like matches,
arches buckle over the dropping saints.
A priest drops the cross.
When I see walls fold inward from the top,
the heavy wooden doors shatter,
I run back into the park.

Stucco houses around the church
spit rubble. A wave of debris knocks
me down. Separated from everyone,
I crawl under a bench, my face caked in dust.
The ringing overpowers me; I rub
my eyes, try to breathe through my mouth.
The sky has vanished, and I beg
the earth to be still.

II.

Once the aftershocks finish,
they count out the family.
Someone asks, *¡María! ¿Dónde está María?*

Before they can argue who will go,
Jorge is running to the church to find her.
He stumbles, trips on rocks.
The ground dips where it didn't before.

The church no longer has a roof;
the steps are smashed to powder.

Out of breath, Jorge calls for his sister
and hears muffled moans from a man in a blue suit
under heavy stones.

The man vomits and bleeds.
Even though Jorge carries him to safety,
the man dies on his back.
He puts the body down outside the church.

He touches stray hands and limbs in rubble,
some stones too big to move.
Jorge doesn't see María, but uncovers more people.

He carries them out,
but none of them were meant to be saved.

III.

I don't know how my brother Jorge found me
in the park, but I hear my name.
He runs to me when I crawl from under
the bench and rubble. I hug him and cry.
My arms pull him tight. He dusts me off.

Jorge carries me in his arms.
I'm trembling, and he doesn't speak.
Ambato is leveled—
the old Spanish buildings gone,
buildings still shifting
and crumbling down.
Our river now flows the wrong way.

The ground's unstable and soft like skin.
Rising black smoke on the next block.
Whoever isn't digging and bawling out names
is too scared to move,
eyes wide, fearing tremors
and the familiar bodies
grouped along each block.

On our street, our family waits around
the table they dragged outside. I imagine
my mother, father; and all our siblings' wet eyes
looking at me like they're seeing my face
for the first time in years.
And when Jorge and I get closer to home,
they run to us.

CHORIZO'S FATHER

Died August 5, 1949

The cornstalks seemed taller
when they found his father in the field.
Only his head stuck out of the dirt,
naturally, as if it grew there.
And Chorizo cried, telling everyone
how he almost tripped over the head.

When Jorge arrived with the priest,
the burro stopped wailing
and kicking in the air, the way everybody
held their breath and gripped doorframes
while the earthquake shook everything.

My brother Jorge said he couldn't forget
the eyes—focused, as if a vision
hit Chorizo's father when the earth
split open like a rib cage,

showing its liver and bowels below
before it snapped shut, taking his body
but leaving the head stranded
in the constant rows of corn.

DIGGING OUT THE CHURCH

In the remnants of our church,
with only one blasted wall intact,
we shovel into the sea of broken blocks
and around the church bell, stripped of its gloss.
While dust floats into our mouths
we shovel and sift downward,
praying to find nothing but more rock and wood.
We don't want to think about our roofless houses,
narrow, broken streets, and the stiff, unmoving limbs
of neighbors buried alive.

Hundreds of us, face down in dust,
wait for the sun, crushed
between stone and lumber,
dirt filled in around us.
Our lungs, lined with the loose bits of land,
shake with the aftershocks.

NEWSPAPER STORY

A typewriter clicks down the headline:
6.9 Earthquake Rocks Ecuador.
They list only numbers: *6,000 dead,*
100,000 homeless, 50 cities rubbled
and destroyed. Stories approved
then put to press. Ink blacks to
white pages, slide through printers.
Newspapers bundled into stacks, hot
to touch. By morning, they're stacked
on street corners before anyone
is awake. Somewhere in the back pages,
the six-line earthquake story waits
with stories of other distant countries.

AFTER THE BROADCAST OF *THE WAR OF THE WORLDS* IN QUITO

Streets fill with barefoot people in pajamas, dragging luggage
and children. They flee to the surrounding heights.
The army and police leave the city to fight Martians in the south.

On the radio, the priest's prayer and church bells interrupted:
*Latacunga's destroyed. Many are dead. Cotocollao is under attack.
They are being wiped out!* Listeners imagine Martians moving
in dark clouds, fire, people collapsing into heaps.

In the station, broadcasters hear sirens, yelling, glass breaking,
and the transmission stops. Radio Quito pleads for calm. Citizens
realize no Martian gas raids or invasion is coming.

They surround the radio station: *Stone them! Burn it! Set it on fire!*
When they throw gas-soaked newspapers, everything, except the brick,
burns. A human chain of people from the third floor breaks,

falls to the pavement, lost in smoke. Twenty people die.
Only the building's facade is saved. Black soot stains
window tops. Nobody ever speaks of it again, and fifty-six years later,
February 12, 1949, is still forgotten in a hiss of static.

LOOKING DOWN THE PASTAZA RIVER

Miles downstream, men search rocky banks
for a boy who surrendered to water, a boy
who comes to the statue of San Martin,
overlooking the bridge outside of town.
The boy listens to the saint's whispers
over the river's roar but hears no voice
or prayer. He leans over the edge and drops.

The current swirls into itself like cocoa.
His body rolls, crashes against rocks.
Searching men poke sticks into weeds, examine
the current's debris, one calling his name.
The boy's face down, tangled in grass
beyond the bridge. The unflinching saint
sits under a cement cross, behind a shrine
littered with burned-out candles.

THE SHAPESHIFTER

In the old clearing, the shaman becomes a jaguar
with the new moon. His writhing body guarded
by leaves and rain falling far from the village.

His eyes close. Drenched body rejects skin.
It swells then tightens. Bones stretch him
to sleeker shape. Black fur bandages him.

His jaws stretch, open to scream into the trees.
Uneven teeth, incisors like stone knives.
Hands tear open into claws,

sinking into mud. Then, silence. Constellations hide
behind clouds. New jaguar's eyes glowing hungry.
He pleases the dark by disappearing.

Undetected, he crunches on bones, drinks the blood
of wicked villagers. He vanishes back into the forest,
like his tracks washed away, swallowed in the downpour.

THE DEER

The way her hands trembled
when they touched the barbwire
stung like frost.
Every time the deer moved,
the fence shook. Neck stuck,

the deer twisted, jerked its legs.
Antlered head pointed
upward, dry mouth sucked air.
She moved without breath.
The deer's eyes quivered,
staring sideways, too impatient

to flinch at her touch.
As she peeled barbs
hooked in skin,
the deer's groan shuddered
like hooves trying to lip ground.
Slow blood blotted fur, touched
her hands like body heat.

She stepped back
to watch the deer stumble away.
The urgency stayed with her
even after her heart stopped racing,
like the scream of life dressed
in the darkness that holds
the fence still and leads it
deeper into the woods.

CURANDERA

I. Eyes Healed with Pullet Feathers

My sister Marcia and I
watch Mamá slide feathers
in an old man's eyes.
She massages his worn eyelids,
then pinches the corners
like kneading dough.
His face is fixed with a throbbing
he almost smiles at.

The old man moves his eyes
free from murkiness.
He stares back at us sitting
on the spiral staircase, our faces
pressed against the railing,
long after Mamá peels away
the cataracts and two pullet feathers.

II. Healing the Kneecap

After falling down the staircase,
my sister Marcia stares
at her backward knee.
Mamá rubs the knee with water:
modest, unmistakable.
Marcia squints, mouths
the saints' names for the jutted bone.
Then, with her hands palmed
to the ground, Marcia screams,
feels Mamá tug the kneecap.
It pops, then slides
into place, leaving Marcia cured,
begging Mamá to stop.

PILLS AND PRAYERS

1950

I. The First Day

To fix my year of no sleep, we follow
old customs. El indígena carries me on his back
to La Merced. Walking behind my mother,
he grunts under my weight. I link my arms
around his neck, bury my face in his poncho.
I feel safe, knowing he won't drop me.
At La Merced, the priest leans my head back

over a basin of holy water. Arabesque pillars
rise about the pulpit. Dug into the walls,
saints' statues frown in stone, gaze into my eyes.
The priest sprinkles water onto my face and neck.
I wince when the prayer for sleep becomes
holy water trickling into my eyes. Instead of sleep,
my eyes sting and blur. The saints' voices
ripple through water and hold me awake.

II. The Next Day

Before sunrise, when clouds drift out of valleys,
we walk through the forests that others fear,
past throat-slit ghosts, hiding demons from the past.
My mother holds my hand, tightens her grip.

She never lets go, and sweat collects in our hands
like blood between our fingers. In a house
in Quito, past familiar roads, my cousin Enrique
gives me pills from China to help the prayers

for insomniacs. That night, I hold the pills
in my mouth. Muscles relax, sag with the bed.
I swallow the heaviness of sleep, and it
seeps into my chest and spreads.

JEWELRY BOX

The jewelry box from Ecuador
is my mother's. Made from bone,
the box edges are carved in rectangles,
rows of laurels. The churches of Quito, drawn

in black lines, hold the box up
on each side: el arco de Santo Domingo,
two steeples of San Francisco, the two churches
with names she can't remember.

On the lid, a monument for la línea
equinoccial framed by the Andes.
A line cuts through hemispheres,
through the globe balanced on bricks.
Inside the box is a cosmos:

her lost lover, insomnia, Ambato's streets
filled with fruits, flowers, dances
to sentimental ballads, tio Adriano's jewelry
on a blanket glistening in sunlight.
She carries the jewelry box

for too many years to count.
The box is worn smooth from the touch
of her hands. Homesickness stays with her
in the miles between her and Ecuador.
She gives them all to me with the box.

II: THE GREEN GOLONDRINA

EATING THE DEAD

Korea, November 25, 1952

Korea is hell. The snow and cold,
so cold we can't give a damn
about anything. My sergeant orders me
to take the enemy corpse
away from camp. I drag the body

the length of the road, and the hill
buzzes like my head. It gets heavier.
The rope tightens. Sergeant tells me
to leave him there, don't bury him
in the frozen ground. I roll him into a ravine.

Before him, the only dead people I saw
were when I was a boy at the four wakes
where the dead lay on the table
for nine days and nights of prayer.
Their eyelids drooped,

hands palms down. The dead stay with me.
I see them everywhere. Once, I saw
a dead bird, dried, smashed in the road.
I wanted to kick it into the brush,
out of my head like skipping rocks
and clumps of dirt.

I never can shake that dead bird—
stinking like moldy rice. The yellow rice,
the chicken mother cooked became the bird's
stale feathers in my mouth. Using her spoon,
she plucked more meat out of the soup.
I chewed obediently while she slid it
onto my plate. Every bite I took
struggled down my throat.

Now, the bodies' slouch, color-faded faces,
waken the dead faces from Puerto Rico.
I never look back, pretending—
just supplies, wood, equipment.
I rub my hands together,
start walking back to camp.

SQUARE DANCE AT KOJE DO REEDUCATION CAMP

Korea, 1952

Behind the statue of Lady Liberty,
holding her torch, the phonograph

spins country. Dancers wear paper masks,
lock arms, and stomp their feet. They dance

on heavy legs, blistered toes. In the back,
lines of men eat soup and rice rations.

Others bundled on the ground under blankets.
The prisoners learn democracy through

the music of scuffed boots. They shiver
like shreds of laundry hanging on sharpened wire.

HOW MY FATHER LEARNED ENGLISH

382nd Hospital, Japan, 1952

The wounded who could not speak English
congregated around the bedridden every morning.
Manuel, the nurse from some other ward,
taught my father and others English
word by word. Sometimes, phrases, the sloppy
repeated English made sense—*Because es porque.*
Porque is because. Dolor es pain, y pain is dolor.
Yo soy es I am. I am. Otra vez, díganme.—
Bee cause. Pain. I am in pain.

English moved my father's tongue unlike Spanish.
It stuck in his mouth, stumbled past his teeth.
He dreamed he forgot Spanish and his tongue
withered away. My father never told anyone
about this or the scratching fear of his legs,
under bandages and scars, never walking again.
He didn't have words in English yet.

LUCÍA

I. Lajas, November '53

His return is like the end of a song.
José the Infantryman now walks
with crutches, but his legs bear
no dirty bandages, red-lined scars.
He scratches at his legs, sometimes
removing metal splinters, pellets.

He sings this song in his sleep:
Every night in Korea, I listened to landscapes.
The breath slid out of our mouths like fire.
Behind me in the dark I felt
dirt explode and cover me in a thin layer.
The ringing moved from ear to ear.

His mother gives him hell
for the next eleven months:
There are no cripples in this house.
You will not be the first.
After she tries to take his crutches away
and stops feeding him decent portions of rice,
José can't stand being at home
or looking in her face.

Instead of sitting with the family for meals,
he wanders beat-up roads and orchards,
stiff crutches riding his armpits
and his stomach groaning
like he's scavenging for food.

II. Lajas, December '53

Josefita, who would die of grief in '82,
knows he came back.
Nevertheless, she waits three weeks
before visiting with her sister,
who carries a bundle of handkerchiefs.
She says, *This is José. I taught him*
how to make handkerchiefs like these
when we were children.
I think he is waking up now.
José shifts in bed, opens his eyes.

His crutches lean against the wall.
He stares at Lucía and hears Josefita say,
Look, here is my wide-eyed sister, Lucía.
In your future, a small dark bird, and in its beak
it will carry a name in black letters
which I am forbidden to see. I cannot see
past the snowdrifts. Never leave her. Never go to Berlin.

After pulling himself up from bed,
José throws his crutches to the floor for her,
and clears his throat: *Thank you, Josefita.*
If you see my mother, tell her
I will not need these damn crutches:
one must learn to walk without limping.

III. Ft. Hood, Texas, October '54

Like all the other yelling matches,
their arguments over fighting and gambling
drag on for hours like rain on tin roofs.
After the passing months teach him
how to walk again, José reenlists, leaves the island,
and Lucía's father takes her to New York City.
What they had withers.

The GIs work amongst heavy-treaded tanks
or in naked fields, with their boots in the sand,
exercising: Attack—Withdraw—Attack—Withdraw.
Off hours, José and others are in town emptying bottles
of rum and getting drunk on Blake Street.
One night they find the tattoo parlor

with the sizzling neon sign and walls full of pictures.
On his left forearm under a white bandage,
José cannot find an ounce of pain
but his first tattoo—sterile lines of ink
needled into skin. The lines make
a black-eyed, red-bodied bird
with a beak locked and holding her name,

its wings arched upward like falling.
The same night, a second tattoo etched
on José's right shoulder. The first time he looks,
there they are: him and Lucía together,
lying in bed, feeding each other mangos.
But when he looks again on his shoulder
there is a green golondrina gliding in rain,
trying to eat butterflies that sink to the earth.
The golondrina never touches the ground.

IV. New York City, January '56

My timing is wrong, Mercedes, José says, stepping on her toes.
This song is too slow. Shoulder to shoulder,
everyone from the block dances in couples
in his sister Mercedes' apartment. This is a party

where dancers pinch their feet into their shoes,
hoping the heat of the room will bring them closer.
Looking around at all the couples, he tells her,
You ought to be ashamed for making me dance.

Lucía dances with an older man, dress hanging off her body.
It's her father who cuts in, *Dance with Lucía,* he says.
José pulls Lucía and smells her perfume. They dance
slow circles, lips almost touching each other's ears.

He asks, *Do you have a boyfriend?*
Do you remember walking through the orchards?
I remember how our eyes met and we kissed
in the green of the leaves.

Lucía squeezes his hand. *You are shaking,* she says.
The couples clap for the song's end. He whispers in her ear,
Like my letters, I won't go away,
and this night will never leave you alone.
I will ask your father for your hand tomorrow.

V. Ft. Devens, Massachusetts, February '58

The last two years have been the same:
José is a training sergeant, and he grinds
the recruits into shape with drills
and formations through the whole week.

Every weekend, he takes a four-hour bus ride
back to the neighborhood like the other boys
going home to families and sweethearts.

Most nights, José stays with Lucía
in the apartment her father pays for.
She always tells him, *Stop staring at me
and go back to sleep.* He can't sleep,
never says anything about his savings
for their wedding next year. He worries
if she's going to ask about money.

The other nights, when they argue
and can't stand the thought of each other,
he stays with his sister, Mercedes,
and sleeps on her couch. She's always asking,
How long can you two go on like this?
He never knows what to say.

On the northbound bus rides
along the coast taking him back to base,
José never falls asleep. He keeps thinking
how their love is stubborn, like battered boats
fighting the current, always threatening to sink.

VI. New York City, February '59

José, three days later, forgets how much
Lucía's father has come to hate him,
forgets his last yelling match with her
that woke up the neighbors, and forgets
the white dress draped on her bed
for their wedding at the church

in the Bronx two days away. Her fingers
drum on the table, the noise pecking at his ears.
Lucía calls him *Imposible*, tells him
to stop fighting with her father, stop
worrying about arguments over money.

And José turns away and shrugs:
Stay with your father. I'm leaving. He steps
out of the apartment, shivers. Snow is falling.
If he turns back, like other times Lucía opened
the window to call to him, he would lean
against the door, begging her to open up.

Walking under a lighted restaurant sign,
which would drop on his niece eight years later,
José turns the corner. Slowly her voice fades,
and her window slams shut, loud enough
to wake up the whole block.
Before she stops calling him,
he tells himself to ignore her voice.
He walks past the shoveled drifts of snow.

VII. New York City, February '59

He carries a picture of four girls
smiling in black dresses.
The last one on the right,
hair dropping into her face
and framing her eyes,
is the one he always studies.
José lets his finger sweep
around her face. He considers
the groaning city, folds
up the picture again.
The girl he always studies
turns out to be Lucía's sister.
Lucía sits next to her—
the coy one with her hair pulled back.

But José will not know this
for another twenty-three years
until returning to Lajas
for Josefita's funeral.
He touches the tattoo
of the golondrina on his shoulder
and gets on the plane
leaving for Berlin.

THE GUARD AT SPANDAU PRISON

Berlin, 1959

I. Arrival to Spandau Prison

Through metal doors,
in white-glove inspected hallways
other guards' footsteps boom.
Somewhere in one of the cell blocks,
I imagine Rudolph Hess, the last prisoner here,
eating, then setting his tray on the ground.
He wipes his mouth
in a handkerchief and lies down.

II. In the Guard Tower

Under steep walls, Hess walks small trails
through snow and dead leaves.
The old man tucks his arms behind his back.
For twelve-hour shifts, I stare into Berlin
past red walls and the ditch coiled in barbed wire.
It's like guarding a monster from the city.
The slow hours are hard on the body—
knees and feet, swollen, throbbing,
and stinging cold, like rifle metal wearing at hands.
I feel the lump of dried quiet in my throat
as he winters the courtyard in silence.

III. The Prison's Past

Every day, I walk past abandoned cells
with gaping doors. Inside, bed skeletons rust,
faucets tarnish in the corners.
The dead prisoners' days gouged
in the walls: chiseled silhouettes of men,

calendars made of never-ending squares,
uneven words and letters telling themselves,
I forgot what the outside looks like.
I want to rub my finger
like a spoon worn to a nub
against the jagged lines in the stone.

IV. Spring

When it grows warmer, the prisoner
works in the garden with precise
columns of flowers and tomato plants.
On his knees, he smoothes the soil
in place with his hands.
He combs his hair the same way.

V. Thirty Years Later

I overlooked Hess's obituary
somewhere in newspaper headlines,
columns, and captions.
I did not see the old photos
of Hitler's number two man
in a Nazi uniform, at Nuremburg,
just before he entered Spandau.

My son told me how the old man
kept that prison up and how after his suicide,
Spandau disappeared like the smoke
of something that never happened.

Through days and nights,
men with sledgehammers
and bulldozers disassembled the prison.
Every scrap of metal was melted
into beams, every tree, wood block, plank
mulched into sawdust,
the bricks crushed to powder.

They shoveled everything into trucks
and hauled Spandau away
from Berlin and to the coast,
all the rubble and debris dumped in the sea.
It wasn't like a funeral when the prison

was scattered in the North Sea
at an unmarked place
like that troubled spot in Berlin
built over with houses, streets,
and buildings where the prison
once stood. It bubbled up in water
then fell through lapping waves.

WHEN MY FATHER WAS IN THE CANAL ZONE

January 9, 1964

For a few days there was a war
in Panama City.
My father was a soldier;
he was thirty-two.
The Panamanians told the gringos
to go home and burned
all the soldiers' downtown homes
to the ground. That's all
he said, so I looked it up
and found a few things.

Protesters scattered down
Fourth of July Avenue
like broken glass.
Tear gas spun from canisters.
When I read about gunshots
and bayonets fixed on rifles,
I tried to fill in the spaces

about formation,
my father's spot in line,
the civilians he hurt.
I thought I could understand
if I read it in a book
or maybe even figure out what
he was thinking
about the clumps of protesters,
the fire drifting and seeping
through buildings and cars,

the sting of knowing what
they yelled in Spanish. Did he feel
any fear pushing back
screaming packs of people
or fear the idea of squeezing his trigger?
Instead of knowing this war,
I see my father in uniform,
a younger man with a rifle at his side,
who says nothing.

PHOBIAS

You rub your hands together and shiver when you tell me the story.
In Panama, every soldier in your unit builds rafts out of branches,
weaves of grass, and ponchos. One at a time,

everyone moves across the Chagres. Your raft, near the center
of the murky current, unravels. Under your breath and river's
   grinding,
you feel something like leeches seep into your clothing

and fill your boots. The young soldier, you call him strong swimmer,
tucks the damp rope in his mouth to drag you
and the remaining bits of raft. Seeing through waves

lapping in my eyes, I imagine myself hearing the silence
then rush of the Chagres, and the kicking ache of my legs struggling
to float. My arms extend, then spear us forward. I know you cannot
   swim,

but the way you tell the story, of how you nearly drowned
without getting your hair wet, makes me taste river froth
spitting down my chin, and see the bank becoming bigger and
   bigger.

After the river devours your hat, the rope braids
into itself and jerks in your hands. You close your eyes
to feel him kick his legs through the current.

SIREN

This woman, her naked body, scoops up
brown water in her hands like fabric,
lets it slide through her hair, down her body,

clinging to her skin. When the American
sees her bathing in the Mekong, he wanders

to the bank, dips his helmet into the water.
A rifle shot cracks. He convulses, falls. Flies

float around him like old friends.
She creeps to the bank, slips into the jungle.

Nearby, another American on lookout sits
on extinct ant piles devoured by the wet season's floods.

He hears only garbled river voices
as he skims a razor across his face,
eyes attentive in a tiny mirror.

MINESWEEP ON HIGHWAY 13 NEAR LAI KEY

1968

Inch by inch, the minesweeper checks the road,
    listening with his feet
        placing his heel then toe down.

    When his detector gleans a claymore,
it hisses, heavies his grip.
    He stops us by holding up his hand.

        The captain tells us to stay off the road.
    We look outward into the trees
and columns of yellow grass. Sometimes, we glance down

    the road at tank tracks, fresh holes
        behind us, claymores he already found.
    And everything still feels lucky

when he pinpoints the spot.
    He sets down the detector and kneels; the headphones
        droop over his helmet, static and clicks in ears.

    We stiffen up when he pulls out his knife,
drags lines around the mine.
    The minesweeper works the blade like he's blind.

        He looks away, and feels blade skimming the sides
    and draw a circle. Metal clinks metal; he moves
the knife under the mine where dirt resumes. As he lifts

    the claymore, no one sees the grenade underneath.
He disappears into a rain of dirt.
    We duck instinctively. Hands cover faces

as dirt and debris falls in a cruel hush. That quiet
      that comes after echoes the blast. Nobody
           ever finds a trace of the minesweeper.

Every day afterward knocks us down
      like every cigarette smoked and smashed under our boots.
      We hold every bite of food

      and bit of water we swallow,
bitterly holding on to the shame of being alive.

THE WET SEASON

Pop nods off through the nights, his hands
sensitive to the rope tied to the sleepwalking soldier.
When dreams take that young man, he rises
to wander through wet leaves and minefields.
The other soldiers, waterlogged, shut their eyes,
lean on tree trunks. Guns glisten in moonlight
through clouds and jungle. They hear every twig
snap and every ant lagging on their ponchos.
Pop yanks him back to sleep. The thud of the soldier,
how everyone stirs and sighs tells him mornings
never come soon enough. Raindrops never stop.

THE FIREFIGHT NEAR NUI BA RA

1968

I thought nothing bothered me
on search and destroy missions.
I closed my eyes and talked to God.
He listened to me when I said prayers
a girlfriend back in Puerto Rico
taught me. I ordered the young soldiers

bunched up at the end to spread out.
The last kid, helmet pressing him down,
vanished under a mortar burst. The sun
stretched the tree line's shadows.
The machine gun nests lashed out
bullets. Taking cover, I saw his shinbone

in the crater's rim. I wanted to touch it,
brush away dirt, carry the bone with me,
but each bullet and explosion buried
the bone deeper, pushed it further away.
I kept saying the prayers and reaching,
hoping they'd keep me alive.

POSTMORTEM

Let's hold hands and walk, kids.
Arriving at Heaven's Gate, we'll say,
Uncle! Auntie! Allow us to go home.
—Vietnamese children's verse

Under the sheet, in the drawer, his purple body
and tight chest held his failed heart.
For seven hours in the city morgue,
Quan the elder was dead

until cold metal on skin woke him.
Starting with clenched teeth cutting into his lips
the blood moved through veins,
air into lungs, memory sparked through his brain.

He felt the silence between his breaths,
how things shift in their sleep,
and footsteps ricochet off distant tiles and repeat.
This chill of night air left ghosts

inside the bones of paling corpses.
The sheet over him kept life
in his body. Quan grew weak and afraid to move.
Beyond the sheet, black fell onto itself
like dark soil shoveled in place.

Unaware of time passing and how it stood
in a quiet hum of ripening life,
voices mingled beyond the dark,
a door opened, and the rush of light
drowned his naked body.

IN YEAR ZERO

Cambodia, 1978

The woman carried her unborn son
through fields of rice paddies
to avoid the roads and patrols.
Skulls surrounded her, their names
chipped in the temples from years
before the Khmer Rouge.
When she stopped under a tree

to rest, eat rice, and drink water,
a ghost of the newly executed
watched her from vines
dangling off the banyan tree.
Then, like needles, the apparition
entered her, tried to push
and take her son from her body.

Food dropped from her hands;
her voice slipped off her tongue
and rose as a groan. She ignored
the ache of her feet, the child's
kicking, and fought the ghost off.
When the child rested,
the apparition joined other ghosts

that drifted through the air
like stretches of white linen
filling in sky. Relieved the baby
was not ready, she resumed walking east
toward Vietnam, passing through
the emptied city of Phnom Penh,
its cracked streets
full of dusty boxes and papers.

THE CLOVERLEAF

The day Pop gets shot, he follows every order and procedure.
He repeats prayers, reads letters from home twice, cleans his
gun. His lieutenant tells him to use the Cloverleaf with five
men to sweep the next mile, to move the unit up. They stem
up, make three-circled sweeps. Pop counts steps, ending
one leaf at the start of the next. Then, on their last loop,
automatic fire traps them, echoes in their helmets, a sound
hot as splintered tree bark. They take cover near the hole
the V.C. stops digging when he hears Pop's patrol.

Bullets rip through air and leaves. Pop doesn't see his
wound until the radioman points to where bullet cleaves past
ligaments, bone, and slides through his shoulder. The tiny
slit drips until his sleeve soaks dark green. *Bullshit*, he yells,
shooting on an emptied clip. They regroup after Kennedy
flanks the V.C. Even Pop shakes his head and looks away
when Kennedy cusses at the corpse. When they withdraw,
Pop leans on McDaniels.

At base camp, pain scrapes into Pop's thoughts. Violet
smoke swirls then fizzles upward with the voices lost in
the propellers. A medic lays him on the gurney, bandages
him up. When the helicopter takes off, McDaniels and the
big black man, whose name Pop forgets, waves. Before he
loses them behind the tree line, Pop watches both relax,
light cigarettes, and study the grass folded under their boots.
He wonders if they'll be alive when he comes back. The
helicopter is cold. He ignores the landscape, the lucky gash
beginning to scar his shoulder.

OBSERVING GRANDFATHER'S WAKE

Lajas, Puerto Rico, 1994

For nine nights, I watched my father pray
with his brothers and sisters. The words unraveled
into several voices. I was too young to pray

with them, but I felt him in every corner of the house.
They stretched their hands over the empty circle
of chairs, the same spot for grandmother's wake

that my father, in Vietnam, missed thirty-five years before.
Their weeping, the scrape of chairs
haunted me. Sweat slid down their faces, like their voices
moving through the house, merging back into one.

Humidity glowed around their bodies like a halo.
On the last night, I couldn't sense him in the house anymore.
The wake ended when someone said alleluia.

GRANDFATHER POSES A FIGHTING COCK

In front of the house, leaning
back on his heels, he holds
the bird away from his body.
My grandfather holds himself tall,
stills the bird's yellow head.
It is not the only one
he raises and takes to Cabo Rojo
every Sunday to drop

into slow-ripping death
while men shout the odds
and slap sweaty money into hands.
For all his birds, he sharpens
spurs, slides them on the claws.
He coaxes the cocks to attack,
flap, and stab the air.

The bird's claws and tail feathers
point up, cut stiff. He dips
his right hand in his pocket,
the cock's shadow
on the white shirt.
His son snaps the photo.

GRANDFATHER'S FIGHTING COCKS

Grandfather trained his birds like this:
every morning he wrapped their claws
in tape and cloth, banded leather over
their beaks, put them

in a ring. He hovered over the birds,
noting good hits when the beak or spurs
struck the heart, jugular, eyes. They sparred
for three- to six-minute intervals.

Other times, he took one bird in both hands,
teased the other into attacking, but he never let
them connect. Then, one at a time, he held
them, poured water onto their exhausted bodies,

and let them rest. The stronger cocks
with one eye, los tuertos, he kept training
for the fights while breeding the blind ones
who once were good fighters. Most nights

grandfather sat under a mango tree in front
of their cages. He slept in his chair
until a cock's crow woke him, stirring him
to return to the sleeping house.

THE ROADS AND SHORTCUTS HOME

The roads and shortcuts home
my father took as a boy were hooded
from moonlight by almond trees.
One night, he heard footsteps

in front of him. He stopped, thought
of the stories viejitos told children
sitting around the stone at the center of town.
Ghost horses dragged chains, chased men

into the deep woods. Jibaro spirits,
displaced and without mouths, walked
the roads, knocked on doors
until the cock's crow at sunrise made

them vanish. Grandfather always told him,
Never run in the darkness
until you know what you are running from.
He heard more footsteps and paused.

My father scraped a match to life, held
it out. He saw the quiet hush of almonds
dropped on the ground by birds that devoured
the flowers above. When the match burned out

on his fingers like the stinging grip
of unseen hands, he felt himself running
through trees and brush, toward the lights
of neighboring houses on that last mile home.

III: WANDERING BETWEEN VILLAGES

PATAPALO THE IMBECILE

> *Any Hispano but a simpleton*
> *would have recognized at once*
> *that this was an invitation to*
> *become a witch, but he innocently*
> *fell into the trap.*
> —Charles Lummis, 1888

I. Patapalo Enters the Desert

Following his guide,
Patapalo doesn't understand
the wisdom the man offers:
thick tongues and languages,
the throbbing of unheard music,
and knowledge of every distant village.

Thousands of mesquite bushes
with rosaries clinging to the thistles
huddle around an adobe.
Patapalo's frozen breaths
float above him as he follows his guide.
People of San Mateo say
the man is like the witches,
for he sleeps with his eyes open.

His fingers prick on thistle.
Patapalo feels blood, rubs
the worn beads of each rosary
carved with Christ's face.
Patapalo's guide knocks
on the splintered door.
The door cracks. His guide says,
We are two. One is ignorant.

II. Patapalo's Skeleton Leaves His Body

The musicians strum
guitars, play their trumpets.
Their music breathes
the dance into everyone
with sweat rolling off skin.

Every note intoxicates him.
Patapalo's feet unwillingly tap
with the rhythm,
and hundreds of witches,
men and women of surrounding towns,
some Patapalo knows,
dance with silhouettes
that stretch to the far side
of the room. Their stamping feet
echo and rumble.

The room shifts with Patapalo.
He claps his hands hard.
The music crowds every
crease of the room and entices
every joint and muscle
until Patapalo's skeleton
slides out of his skin
and joins the witches and shadows.

III. Patapalo Kisses the Goat

In the line of people disappearing
in white light at the end of the room

Patapalo watches the others kneel
and kiss the goat's coarse tail.

The goat's body stands upright.
He faces away from the people,

and his open mouth never speaks,
beard tangled, dark and pointed.

When the goat gets closer, Patapalo stares
at the horns weaved and curled like gold.

Then, Patapalo finds himself lowered
near the hooves, bathed in sin.

His nose twitches, fills
with the overwhelming smell of shit.

He presses his lips on the fur,
convinced he is kissing a king.

IV. Patapalo and the Tongue of Wisdom

The others receive
the tongue of wisdom,
and Patapalo's legs shake,
the large snake slithers
around, clutching him.
He hears its jaws open.
The snake moves its tongue
between his lips—
pink skimming past his teeth
and resisting Patapalo's tongue.

Patapalo's eyes roll back.
The tongue down
his throat flicks and spreads.
Knowledge seeps
through his blood,
and brain. Patapalo can sense
everything moving
like the words crawling
on his own skin.

Because he could not breathe
or stop being afraid, Patapalo yells,
Jesus, Mary, and Joseph!
All vanish as he slumps
to the ground, wheezing for air.
The breath stays
in Patapalo's mouth.

V. Patapalo the Imbecile Leaves the Desert

Patapalo finds himself alone,
the smell of sulfur
dying away in the wind.

He walks past rocks, slumped cacti,
and the mesquite bushes
stripped of rosaries and thistles.

He lags toward his village, staring out,
baffled about the black magic that gives him
wisdom and takes it away,
when he speaks the three holy names.

Patapalo's lips pucker, trying to whistle
the witch songs he loses
with every step out of the desert.

HANDSOME FRANCISCO ANSURES VISITS THE MORALES SISTERS

San Rafael, New Mexico, 1885

Somehow, the Morales Sisters scared Francisco
into having coffee that morning, and they
scolded him about vanity, how men

need to rely less on their masculine qualities.
He laughed with them, tasted a hint of metal
with each sip. His hands shook, spilled his cup.

Once the heat spread from his hands,
into his skin, he rushed home
with the sisters' laughter behind him.

He ran past his wife into the bathroom.
In the mirror, he watched stubble fall out,
skin smooth, Adam's apple sink into his throat.

Francisco scratched his scalp; hair grew
two feet longer. Breasts swelled with every breath.
He sobbed, mouth agape when he felt his penis

vanish into his groin. When Mrs. Ansures
opened the door, she screamed. His voice
became softer, and every time he spoke,

his wife cried, *What have you done, Francisco?*
Who did this to you? He screeched, *Don't look at me!*
The Morales brujas have changed me. Help me!

They both were powerless, wondering how long
they'd have to scrape and save to pay
these same witches and beg them to lift his curse,

wondering how the witches would grind and mix
herbs with animal parts into a smoking brew
that Francisco would have to suck down like a dog.

BEATRIZ DE LOS ANGELES

New Mexico, 1637

> *Much of the Santa Fe community*
> *lived in fear of displeasing her.*
> *When one of her lovers, Diego Bellido,*
> *started a quarrel and beat her, she fed him a*
> *bowl of bewitched corn gruel. He shortly fell ill*
> *and passed away after several weeks of agony.*
> —Marc Simmons,
> *Witchcraft in the Southwest.*

I want to make you howl in pain, feel
the potion pierce infections into your guts.

I've studied your nightly routine:
a drunken walk through the darkened town

to my house, loud knocks against the door,
a fuming temper. But I am not

one of your whores. I have seduced others,
and I won't wait for you or any man to bury me.

And who are you, Diego, writhing wildly,
refusing to die? That bowl of corn gruel

I fed to you should remind you of the bruises
throbbing on my face and neck.

It was only passing anger and booze, you say;
I call it your mistake. Now you clench your hands,

roll and crash yourself against the floor—
the only way to make sure you pay.

My potions wear away at you, so I'll watch
you for weeks, clutching your stomach

until my bruises vanish. Then I'll leave your corpse
dangling on a fence on the way into town.

UNEARTHING SKELETONS AT THE PUYÉ RUINS

1934

From the Ildefonso Pueblo, the men ride
in pickups for good wages, meager lunches,
hands rubbed raw, days full of work. They know
the stories of the dead returning to life but still they go.
Out in blustery heat, where the archaeologist points,
Ildefonso men spade and shovel the site.
Skeletons begin to shiver and stir:
Don't take me out. Don't take me out.

The excavation reveals rotted walls, fire pits,
the field of graves. When the first man finds
a skeleton, he pulls away from its grip and yells.
He pales, collapses dead. With the stunned
crew hauling him home, they eye
the skeleton who clawed into the digger's feet.

From holes and deepening trenches
come spewing dust, routine scrapes of shovels,
men hauling boxes of dirt. From Ildefonso men,
who flee to higher ground, come terrified voices,
bawling at newfound skeletons. Clouds darken
the sun. Some men begin to vomit.
Skeletons plead, *Don't take me from this ground.*

At the mesa's excavation site, the skeletons
assault every Ildefonso man. From the guilt and fear
worming inside them, they stop digging.
The archaeologist takes what he can, crating
the dead's secrets, and shipping them away.
The Ildefonso men return for good, carrying
to their dwindling village a plague
from Puyé skeletons unearthed and stirred to life.

THE LOSS OF JUAN PEREA'S EYES

Every night, Juan Perea becomes
a cat. He inserts borrowed eyes
into his sockets, and on the table,

he rests his eyes in a saucer.
Assuming cat's tail, body arch,
he tiptoes between houses.
He recites hexes burned

into his memory and tongue
like cooked cat bones.
He leaves curses at houses:

worms poisoning food, mice growing
inside stomachs, the stealing
of a man's beating heart.

One morning, he returns home,
drops to his knees, sees
the upturned table,
hungry dog eating his eyes.

ON JUAN'S CAPTURE OF SEÑORA CHONITA

1897

In a dirt-drawn circle, Juan waits
for nightfall. The old people say
boys and men, blessed with the name Juan,
hold the power to catch witches.

To trap Señora Chonita, he wears
an inside-out shirt like superstitious travelers
afraid of her curses. While he scratches
his neck red, eyes adjusting to dusk,

a coyote noses into the plaza,
the way witches become orbs of light
wandering between villages.

The coyote sees him, sniffs the air,
enters the circle. Juan yells, *¡Venga, bruja!*
The coyote panics and shakes, fur melting
to cold naked skin. She crouches,

squints at him. Juan never stops fearing
Señora Chonita even when townspeople,
clutching torches and bullied prayers, loom

over her just before they kill her. Forever after
Juan is trapped, like a witch in a circle,
afraid of feeling the grip of clawed hands
dragging him into the desert.

MICTLANTECUHTLI

Mictlantecuhtli's name evokes fear: skeletal god
of death and the underworld, Mictlan,
the place of silence away

from the world's toils. The Aztecs depict him
dressed in human bones, offer him the flayed skins
of men and women. On his haunches, he sits
on the balls of his feet, crosses his thin arms
across his chest, contemplating the futures of souls.

His eyes may be white like fog, but he can
peer through darkness, watch you
like his owls, bats, and spiders. Reluctant

to release you, Mictlantecuhtli sends you
on tasks around the underworld, gives
you broken instruments to play,
and orders his minions to dig pits to trap you.
Never turn your back to Mictlantecuhtli

or trust his words. You will fall deeper
into Mictlan, beyond the light of his inextinguishable
fires, and shatter like dried bones.

VIRACOCHA LEAVES TO THE WEST

Viracocha made the earth, the stars, the sky and
mankind, taking to his wanderings as a beggar,
teaching his new creations the rudiments of
civilization, as well as working numerous miracles.
        — from *Lords of Cuzco* by Burr Brundage

Knowing he created the earth and stars, Viracocha
walked through the mountains toward
the coast. He never looked back; his beard and cloak

swayed with the wind, thick as spun wool.
He never rested, never succumbed to hunger
or the elements. Viracocha passed through
valleys, where rivers flowed from living stone,

the same stone he used to carve men. He gave
his tribes names, knowledge, crops.
Some say he was taunted, driven from hidden villages
in the jungles. He never inflicted vengeance
except for leaving, abandoning his creations

to survive like naive children wandering
the woods. Some watched him stand in the surf,
the froth of the sea. Viracocha walked slowly
on the waters to the west, fading
from their sight like prophesies of his return.

NAZCA LINES

1534

Between two rivers, Pedro Cieza de Leon
and his men walk the desert plateau.
Each footstep groans and grates rock
into earth. The Spaniards lug barrels, sacks of flour,
sugar, spears; their swords drag at their sides.
Two indígenas, with ropes cutting their waists,
haul a cannon. Flags shriek in the wind

like splitting tongues. In this desert, they pass
stacks of rock and Inca trails that stretch
over mountains and into craggy horizons.
The sun throbs on breastplates and helmets
as layers of heat rise and float through them.
Dust mixes with the sweat that drips

down forehead lines, noses, and into eyes.
Walking with his head down, Cieza de Leon
imagines thriving towns they left in the north,
rich valleys, the gushing sound of rivers,
and sloped fields of crops
on the mountains that interrupt desert.
The horizon never changes, never grows larger;
the sun shifts to the west.

All around, grazed lines, no more
than a few inches deep or wide, created
from black volcanic pebbles scraped away
to reveal a base of yellow sand and clay.
Everything is preserved by the desert

like pauses between conversations.
Cieza de Leon stops to drink water. He ignores
the guide, who tells him, *The gods,*
los Viracochas, made these lines.

1926

On flights between Lima and Arequipa,
the pilot of the Stinson-Faucett
takes passengers over the desert.

Nine thousand feet up,
everything vibrates. The blaring propeller
makes solid circles. His eyes scan
the cloudless sky, then slant downward.

The pilot spots the strange marks in the land
other pilots gossip about.
Some dismiss them as foolish Indian stories

and others think they're graveyards.
He sees enormous intricate shapes,
like the spirals falling into themselves.

Lines, wide like runways, narrow
then bend before continuing into valleys
and over the mountains. Soon, empty deserts
and mountains will resume.

The passengers breathe in the humming
stale cabin air, and the pilot
wants them to see but says nothing.

1939

She spends weeks at a time
in the desert, living off
fruit, nuts, and water.
For decades, Maria Reiche
sweeps rocks from
the miles of lines,
keeping them clean and intact
like the ancient hands
that dug them into the dirt.

Nearby, a basket holds
pencils, paper,
spools of string and rope.
Her camera loaded on a tripod.
All around her, piles of rocks
and the overlapping lines

are layered by silence and heat.
Like every day, morning fog
slides off the plateau
and into the river valleys.
Maria stands on a hill,
measures the lines with her binoculars
and pencils marks in her notebook.

On the summer solstice
during sunrise,
light fills the lines,
connects 450 yards of clay.
Life grows from the land.
A bird like a phoenix emerges,
wings spread in flight,
feathers gapped.

In this isolation, her breath escapes her.
And other shapes, the blue whale,
monkey, spider, hummingbird
scraped into the plateau,
still sleep like bones and potshards
under the stars and sun.

ABOUT THE AUTHOR

Juan J. Morales was born in the U.S., but he has extended family in Ecuador and Puerto Rico, and he grew up hearing family stories that inspired much of the poems in *Friday and the Year That Followed*. Juan received his MFA from the University of New Mexico in 2005. His poetry has appeared in *Blue Mesa Review, Borderlands: Texas Poetry Review, Poet Lore,* and *War, Literature, and the Arts.* He teaches English at Pueblo Community College in Pueblo, CO, where he lives with his wife, Lauren. This is his first collection of poetry.

A NOTE ON
OSWALDO GUAYASAMÍN

Oswaldo Guayasamín was born in Quito, Ecuador, on July 6, 1919. He graduated from La Escuela de Bellas Artes in Quito as painter and sculptor; he is considered one of the great master artists of Ecuador. His images capture the political oppression, racism, poverty, and class division found in much of South America. His work has been shown in museums in all capitals of America and in many countries in Europe: in the State Hermitage in Saint Petersburg, and in galleries in Moscow, Prague, Rome, Madrid, Barcelona, and Warsaw. During his lifetime, he carried out 180 individual exhibits, and his production was fruitful in paintings, murals, sculptures, and monuments. Guayasamín also built a museum in Quito that features his work. He died on March 10, 1999, when he was 79 years old. For more information, please visit the Fundación Guayasamín at http://www.guayasamin.com.

ABOUT THE PUBLISHER

Bedbug Press was founded in 1995 by Tony Gorsline, who has had a lifelong love of books and writing. Under the imprints Cloudbank Books and Fairweather Books, Bedbug Press has published twelve books of poetry, a creative non-fiction memoir, and a series of children's coloring books.

In 2003, the press established The Northwest Poetry Series with the publication of *My Problem with the Truth* by Chris Anderson. Since then three more books by Northwest poets have been added to the series: *Insects of South Corvallis* by Charles Goodrich, *Out of Town* by Lex Runciman, and *A Bride of Narrow Escape* by Paulann Petersen.

Also in 2003, the press began an annual poetry contest, The Rhea & Seymour Gorsline Poetry Competition. The contest offers a cash prize and publication of the winning manuscript. *Textbook Illustrations of the Human Body* by George Estreich (Corvallis, OR) was the winner of the 2003 contest. *Solar Prominence* by Kevin Craft (Seattle, WA) was the 2004 winner, and *Gathering Sound* by Susan Davis (Chapel Hill, NC) and *Friday and the Year That Followed* by Juan J. Morales (Pueblo, CO) were co-winners of the 2005 prize.

Bedbug Press authors have received a number of honors: Barbara Koons *(Night Highway)*, first finalist for the 2006 Best Books of Indiana Awards; David Hassler *(Red Kimono, Yellow Barn)*, 2006 Ohio Poet of the Year; Paulann Petersen, recipient of the Stewart H. Holbrook Literary Legacy Award and a finalist for the 2006 Oregon Literary Arts Oregon Book Awards for Poetry; Dorinda Clifton *(Woman in the Water: A Memoir of Growing Up in Hollywoodland)*, featured at the 2006 Memphis Film Festival and recipient of a fellowship to the MacDowell Colony.

It is our hope that all our books express a commitment to quality in writing and publishing. Please visit www.bedbugpress.com for more information about the press.

COLOPHON

Titles and text are set in Hiroshige Book.
Title page titles are set in Presscon Roman.

Typeset by ImPrint Services, Corvallis, Oregon.